THE GOOD FIGHT

STORIES ABOUT REAL HEROES

NONFICTION BY
TOD OLSON

SCHOLASTIC INC.
New York   Toronto   London   Auckland   Sydney
Mexico City   New Delhi   Hong Kong

COVER PHOTO BY
REEBOK YOUTH IN ACTION AWARD

Copyright © 1999 by Scholastic Inc.
All rights reserved. Published by Scholastic Inc.
Printed in the U.S.A.

ISBN 0-439-05715-9

SCHOLASTIC, READ 180, and associated logos and designs are trademarks and/or registered trademarks of Scholastic Inc. LEXILE is a trademark of MetaMetrics, Inc.

6 7 8 9 10   23   06 05 04

TABLE OF CONTENTS

INTRODUCTION

Everyone has a hero. It could be an athlete—someone with amazing talent on the court or the field. It could be a movie star with great looks and a glamorous life.

Maybe your hero made millions in business and owns everything you could ever want. Or maybe he or she is a politician who got elected against all odds.

This book is about heroes of a different kind. It's about six people who noticed that something wasn't right and decided to do something about it.

Some fought for their own freedom, some for other people's lives. Two died for their causes. The others were lucky to escape alive.

They did their work in different times—from the 1870s to the present. But they all had one thing in common: They weren't afraid to stand up and say "No" while almost everyone else was silent.

A Native American chief outwitted the U.S. army for three months, trying to find freedom for his people.

CHIEF JOSEPH

1841–1904

Tuekakas had been chief of a group of Nez Perce Indians for years. But in 1871, he became gravely ill and didn't expect to recover. He called his son Joseph to his bedside and gave him final words of advice.

"A few more years, and white men will be all around you," warned Tuekakas. "They have their eyes on this land. My son, never forget my dying words. This country holds your father's body. Never sell the bones of your father and your mother."

A few months later, Tuekakas died. His band of Nez Perce needed a new chief. And 30-year-old Joseph was their choice.

It was a difficult time to be chief. All through the West—from North Dakota to Nevada—Native Americans were losing their land. Some fought with all their strength and died in battle. Others went quietly to reservations—patches of dry land set aside for them by the government.

So far, Joseph and his Nez Perce had been lucky. They still lived free on their ancestors' land. But time was running out. White settlers were closing in, and

Joseph was pushed closer and closer to the most important decision he would ever make: Should he risk his life for his people's freedom?

As the new chief, Joseph did his best to make peace with the white settlers. He made friends with his new neighbors. He met with government officials and tried to make a deal to save his land.

But in May of 1877, the axe fell. A United States general, Oliver Otis Howard, ordered Joseph and several other chiefs to come to a council.

A leader named Toohoolhoolzote did the talking for the Nez Perce. He wasn't known for being shy, and before long Howard tried to silence him.

Toohoolhoolzote was furious. "Who are you that you ask us to talk, and then tell me I shall not?" he demanded. "Are you the Creator? Did you make the world? Did you make the rivers run? Did you make the grass grow? [Is that why you feel that you can] talk to us as though we were boys?"

General Howard answered by throwing Toohoolhoolzote in jail. And he told the Nez Perce that they all had to move to a reservation in 30 days.

Joseph rode home. When he arrived, U.S. soldiers were already there. The Nez Perce were outnumbered, and they decided they had to give in.

"We were like deer. They were like grizzly bears," Joseph said about the settlers. "We had a small country.

Their country was large. We were content to let things remain as the Great Spirit made them. They were not, and would change the rivers and mountains if they did not suit them."

Joseph's people packed up and headed south toward a reservation. But on the way, several angry young warriors disobeyed orders—and put the entire tribe in grave danger. They sneaked off and killed four white settlers.

The Nez Perce knew it was just a matter of time before the soldiers would track them down. And the soldiers would be looking for revenge.

The Indians camped in a canyon and waited.

General Howard sent some volunteers after the Nez Perce. Then he wired a message to his superiors. "Think we will make short work of it," he bragged.

The volunteers arrived at Joseph's camp. The Nez Perce could see that they were outnumbered again. This time it was two-to-one.

The Nez Perce sent out a group with a white flag, signalling that they wanted to talk.

But in response, the soldiers opened fire.

And they were soon sorry that they did.

The Nez Perce held their ground. Bullets and arrows flew through the air. When the dust settled, the Nez Perce had wiped out a third of the soldiers. The rest of the soldiers ran for their lives.

"I have been in lots of scrapes," an army scout remembered years later, "but I never went up against anything like the Nez Perce in all my life."

News of the battle traveled fast around the country. People were stunned to hear how easily the soldiers were beaten. General Howard was embarrassed. He called for more troops and set out after Joseph.

Joseph and the other chiefs gathered their ragged group of 250 warriors, 450 women and children, and 2,000 horses. They headed east for the hunting lands of Montana and Wyoming.

In the next three months they would lead the U.S. Cavalry on a 1,700-mile chase. It was one of the most amazing pursuits in American history.

The Nez Perce climbed mountains and wound through canyons. They outwitted the soldiers every chance they got. They used the forest for cover and hid among boulders. Every time an army scouting party got too close, Nez Perce sharpshooters picked them off.

In July, they had a close escape. They reached Montana's Bitteroot Mountains and camped in a canyon. U.S. troops managed to block the narrow pass out of the canyon, and it looked like the Nez Perce would have to surrender.

But the Indians had a plan. Warriors climbed up to the ridge of the canyon. They formed a long line, and Joseph moved all the women and children out behind them. By the time the soldiers realized what was happening, it was too late.

The Nez Perce turned south, still hoping to find good hunting country. Early in August, a company of drunken soldiers caught up with them and ambushed the Native Americans on a high plateau. They killed 80 people—half of them women and children—before the warriors could respond.

The chase went on, mile after mile, week after week. Soon the Nez Perce had only one hope. They had to make it to Canada.

So Joseph led his people north. On September 29, they stopped for rest, just 40 miles from the safety of the border. The Nez Perce knew that General Howard was two days' journey south. They decided to take a chance and stop to hunt buffalo in the morning. But they did not know that the cavalry of Colonel Nelson "Bear Coat" Miles was just north of their camp.

At dawn, Joseph's people awoke to the sound of 600 horses thundering across the plains. They fought to a standoff. But by the end of the day, they were completely surrounded.

For five days, they held the soldiers off. Then finally, Joseph appeared under a white flag, walked into Colonel Miles's camp, and handed over his gun.

"I am tired of fighting," Joseph told the Colonel. "The old men are all dead. My people, some of them, have run away to the hills and have no blankets, no food. No one knows where they are—perhaps freezing to death. I want to have time to look for my children. Maybe I shall find them among the dead. Hear me, my chiefs! I am tired. My heart is sick and sad. From where the sun now stands I will fight no more forever."

Chief Joseph never got to search for his people. The generals sent the Nez Perce to a prison in Kansas and then to a dry patch of land in Oklahoma's Indian Country. Along the way, most of them died of hunger and disease.

Two years later, Joseph went to Washington, D.C. to tell U.S. Congressmen about the sad fate of his people. "You might as well expect the rivers to run backward as that any man who was born a free man should be content when penned-up," he told them.

Chief Joseph was sent back to Indian Country and then to a reservation in Washington state, where he died in 1904. He never saw the land that "holds his father's bones" again.

Do you think that Chief Joseph was a hero? Why or why not?

During World War II, one young woman risked her life to save her friends.

IRENE GUT OPDYKE

BORN 1921

It was September of 1939. Irene Gut was 18 years old and had her life ahead of her. She was about to start nursing school near her home in Radom, Poland. When she finished, she'd get a good job. Her future looked bright.

Then, in just a few days, World War II swallowed her life.

Just before Irene's school started, Germany invaded Poland from the west. The Russian army attacked from the east.

Bombs began to fall on the very first day of classes. Houses burned to ashes. People lay in pools of blood on the street.

Panicked, Irene fled into the forest.

But there, instead of finding safety, she was attacked by Russian soldiers.

She awoke in a hospital far from home. She had no idea if anyone in her family had survived. She was alone and scared.

Irene would soon learn that her life as she knew it was over. The seven-year nightmare of World War II was just beginning. The German army had taken over half of Europe, including Poland. Their soldiers ruled the country with an iron fist. Anyone suspected of opposing them could be thrown into jail without a trial—or even killed. But even in the midst of this terror, Irene Gut risked her life again and again to save friends who were in danger.

Early in 1941, Irene left the hospital. But it wasn't long before German soldiers caught her. They stuffed her in a boxcar with other prisoners and sent her to a Polish town called Tarnopol. There she was put to work in a weapons factory.

Irene didn't stay long. She was attractive, with blonde hair and blue eyes. And her good looks caught the attention of a German major named Eduard Rugemer. The major got her a job cooking and cleaning in the officers' quarters nearby.

Irene was safe for now. But she was surrounded by danger. From the window of the officers' quarters, she watched German soldiers patrol the streets.

One day, she witnessed a terrifying scene. A German soldier lost his temper and beat several Jews to death. Irene started to scream but the major put his hand over her mouth. "Terrible things happen to Jew-lovers," he said to her.

As Irene knew, German dictator Adolf Hitler and his political party, the Nazis, had a crazed hatred of the Jewish people. Under his orders, Jews were forced into crowded, run-down neighborhoods called ghettos. They were sent to labor camps where they worked as slaves. And that was only the beginning.

It was illegal for anyone to help the Jews. Anyone caught assisting a Jew could be shot on sight, or hanged as an example to everyone else.

But Irene ignored Major Rugemer's warning. She got to know 12 Jews who worked in the laundry room. And she began to help them out.

She cooked for the German officers and served them food. While they stuffed themselves with roast duck and wine, she stole butter, bread, and fruit for her friends.

In time, she began to pass on something much more valuable: information.

In the summer of 1943, Irene overheard the German officers talking about the "liquidation of the Jews." She listened in horror as they discussed the plan. They were going to round up all the Jews and send them to camps. There, the Jews would be worked to death or killed immediately. The terrible results of this plan are known today as the Holocaust.

As the plans developed, Irene kept her friends in the laundry room informed. They told Jewish workers in the factory, and many escaped to the forest. But time was running out for the others.

One summer day, the Nazis started rounding up

Jews. German policemen herded them through town. They beat anyone who stumbled or fell behind.

Irene watched while a German soldier tore a baby from its mother's arms and threw the infant down on the cobblestones. When the mother rushed for her child, a bullet tore through her skull.

Another Polish man was shot when he tried to pull a woman and child from the group.

A rabbi was beaten to death while he knelt reciting the Jewish prayer for the dead.

The grim parade passed through town. Then Irene heard the air explode with gunfire. The Nazis shot hundreds of Jews that day and buried their bodies in shallow graves.

"I witnessed the nightmare of my life," Irene would say much later. "I wanted to strangle these human beasts. I went home that night and asked, 'Where are you, God?'"

The next morning, she knew she had to act. The major had just moved into a new home and taken Irene with him. There, she found a hidden cellar and told her friends from the laundry room about it. She left the door to a coal chute open. One by one, her 12 friends arrived in the night to hide—right under the nose of Major Eduard Rugemer.

For months they lived this way. The 12 fugitives came upstairs during the day to help Irene prepare for the major's parties. At night they went back to their damp home in the cellar. There they sat in silence, listening to the officers eat, drink, and laugh overhead.

But the war was not done with Irene. Later in the year, she was forced to watch the hanging of two families. A Christian family had been caught trying to help a Jewish family, and this was their punishment.

All the way home she kept hearing their cries. She was so disturbed that she left the major's cellar door open by mistake.

That afternoon, Major Rugemer walked in and discovered that his home had been turned into a hiding place for Jews. He went straight for the telephone to call the German police.

Irene followed him and knelt, holding onto his legs. "Please, please let them live," she pleaded. He put the phone down. He didn't want to see her dead, he said. He disappeared for an hour to think.

When the Major returned, he told Irene he would protect her secret. In exchange, Irene would have to agree to be his companion. "It was a small price to pay for that many lives," Irene said later.

By the next spring, the Germans were beginning to lose the war. They evacuated Tarnopol. Irene found her friends a hiding place in the forest.

After the war, Irene found her way to the United States. She kept her story private until 1980, when a newspaper story caught her eye. The article told of people who claim that the Holocaust never happened—that the Nazis did not, in fact, kill six million Jews during World War II.

Irene decided she had a message that people needed to hear. She began touring the country to speak in schools, churches and synagogues.

Children, she says, have to stand up to racism, because if they don't, who will? "If you think only with your head, not with your heart," she says, "the head will tell you, 'Oh, that's dangerous, don't do this.' So you have to involve your heart."

Why do you think that Irene made the choices she did—even though she was putting herself in serious danger?

A nature writer told Americans to care for the environment as though their lives depended on it.

RACHEL CARSON

1907–1964

In the fall of 1962, millions of Americans sat down to read a brand new horror story.

It began with an imaginary scene: "There was once a town . . . where all life seemed to live in harmony with its surroundings."

Then suddenly, a strange plague came. It left birds, farm animals, pets, even people, dead. Spring arrived, but there was nothing but silence. "No witchcraft, no enemy action had silenced the rebirth of new life," the book explained. "The people had done it themselves."

The book was called *Silent Spring,* and it warned of a great disaster. It claimed that chemicals used to kill weeds and insects were slowly poisoning the earth.

The author, Rachel Carson, was a quiet, best-selling nature writer. But her book started a huge controversy. Big businesses were making millions on these chemicals. And they had powerful politicians as allies. Carson stood up to them all.

In the process, she changed the way Americans think about nature. Carson claimed that nature has its own delicate balance. And people, she said, are just another part of nature. When humans try to control the natural world by killing off animals or plants, they upset the balance. And that puts the entire earth in danger.

"Thanks to a woman named Rachel Carson," the *Saturday Evening Post* announced in September 1962, "a big fuss has been stirred up to scare the American public out of its wits."

Rachel Carson was an unlikely rebel. Born in 1907, she was a bookish kid. When she got tired of reading, she liked to wander in the woods. She wrote stories and poems. She sold an essay to a children's magazine for three dollars before her twelfth birthday.

In college, Carson studied science and became fascinated with the ocean. When she graduated, she wrote radio shows for a government agency that kept watch over the ocean, lakes, and rivers.

One day, her boss told her that one of her scripts just wouldn't work. It was too good for them, he said. He suggested she submit it to the *Atlantic Monthly*, a big national magazine.

So the September, 1937 issue of the *Atlantic* included an essay titled simply, "Undersea." Carson's career as a writer had begun.

She then wrote a series of books about the mysteries of the ocean. She described the lives of fish and plants and coral. And she did it in such a way that all readers could share her love of the sea.

In 1951, the second of these books hit the best-seller list. It stayed there for 18 months. Rachel Carson had a special gift. She could turn complex science into poetry. And it made her famous. Still, as she told a friend, she felt more comfortable in sneakers at the shore than in high heels at a reception.

In 1957, she was living in Maine, wandering the shore in sneakers. She got a letter from a friend named Olga Owens Huckins, who lived in Massachusetts. Huckins reported that the government had sprayed the coastline with DDT, a powerful poison.

The government had been trying to kill mosquitoes. But Huckins said the spray also killed the birds in her yard. "All of these birds died horribly and in the same way," she wrote. "Their bills were gaping open, and their claws were drawn up to their breasts in agony."

Rachel began to make phone calls. As she dug up information, she realized she'd uncovered a serious scandal. The people who had okayed the use of these chemicals didn't understand the damage they could cause. Or maybe they just didn't care.

Carson decided she had to write a book. She dove into the project. She called scientists and dug into government papers. She gathered files of research.

Her health kept getting in the way. First she got the flu, then an ulcer. Finally, in 1960 came the worst blow of all. Doctors told Rachel that she had cancer. She could die in a year, they said.

The news sent her back to work with a passion. Often she typed in her bed or in her wheelchair. Finally, by the beginning of 1962, she had finished her book.

That book, *Silent Spring*, told a terrible tale. For two decades, the government had been covering farms, gardens, forests, and homes with poisonous sprays. The goal was to kill insects that eat crops or spread disease. But according to *Silent Spring*, the chemicals also killed helpful creatures.

The chemicals also threatened *people*. The poisons found their way into drinking water through rivers and streams. They got into the bodies of cows and chickens that were raised for meat. Eventually they ended up in the bodies of people everywhere.

As soon as *Silent Spring* came out, the chemical companies went on the attack. One group of companies paid $250,000 to produce a booklet saying Carson was wrong. A state official in New Jersey said Carson was "part of a nature-balancing, organic-gardening, bird-loving, unreasonable citizenry." Others claimed that no woman could understand the science behind chemical sprays.

Carson watched most of the battle from her home in Maine. Her cancer had gotten worse. But on April 3, 1963, she gathered the strength to appear on TV.

A huge audience watched Carson defend her book. For more than a century, she said, people had gotten carried away with their ability to dominate nature.

The awesome powers of science had created trains, planes, telephones, electricity, nuclear power, and more. But now, Carson said, it was time to admit that technology has its limits.

People had to realize that the earth is a fragile system, she insisted. And humans need to protect it in order to survive. "We still haven't become mature enough to think of ourselves as only a tiny part of a vast and incredible universe," she said. "We have [the] power to alter and destroy nature. But man is a part of nature and his war against nature is . . . a war against himself."

In the end, Carson's supporters were louder than her critics. Her book rose to the top of the best-seller lists. By the end of 1962, 40 states were considering laws to control the use of insect sprays.

Even more important, the world had proof that progress came with a high cost. People began to realize that nature must be protected. Environmental groups began to form around the country. Many of them were inspired by Rachel Carson.

In September of 1963, Rachel and a friend went out to a rocky point near her house in Maine. There they watched a stream of monarch butterflies heading south for the winter, never to return. She later wrote to her friend, saying she felt no sadness that the butterflies lead such short lives. "When any living thing has come to the end of its cycle, we accept that end as natural." It is, she added, "not an unhappy thing that a life comes to its end."

Rachel Carson died of cancer seven months later, on April 14, 1964. "It is good to know," she had written the year before, "that I shall live on even in the minds of many who do not know me and largely through association with things that are beautiful and lovely."

List the different technologies you use in your life. What are the good sides to them? The bad sides? How would your life be different without them?

In 1951, a 16-year-old girl decided that her school should be as good as those the white kids attended.

BARBARA JOHNS

1934–1991

By the winter of 1950, going to school had become a struggle for Barbara Johns. Every day she boarded an aging bus handed down by the white schools in her Virginia town. If she was lucky, the bus made it all the way to R.R. Moton, her segregated black high school.

Once there, she had to cope with the bad condition of her school. Half the classes took place in tar-paper shacks that were sometimes mistaken for a chicken farm by travelers. The buildings leaked and offered little protection against the cold. "The man who drove the bus—who was also my history teacher—had to make fires in the shacks each morning to keep us warm," Johns recalled later.

Barbara was a junior at the time. And her experience was shared by black kids all across the American South. Laws in Southern states kept African Americans from sharing public facilities with white people. The system was called segregation. And it meant separate waiting rooms at bus stations, separate bathrooms, separate water fountains, and of course, separate schools. And the facilities weren't just separate. The ones for whites were always better.

Still, Barbara had done pretty well with what she had. She joined the drama group, the chorus, and the student council. She also traveled to white schools where students did not have to use the auditorium for gym classes. She saw that sick kids had infirmaries, and hungry kids had cafeterias.

One day, some boys came back from visiting a white school, talking about how nice it was. Something in Barbara snapped. "I kept thinking about it all the way home," she remembered. "I thought about it while I was in bed that night, and I was still thinking about it in the morning."

Soon after, at age 16, Barbara Johns thought of a plan. She would stand up and fight for a better school. Her protest attracted the attention of leaders who were attacking segregation across the South. And Barbara became part of one of the most important Supreme Court cases in American history.

Johns started by planning small, secret meetings with other student leaders. At first, they weren't trying to attack segregation. She and the others simply wanted what they deserved: a decent school.

During the winter of 1950 to 1951, the students started going to school board meetings. But their suggestions were ignored, and they realized that the board was not going to improve their school. So, on

April 23, 1951, they decided to take matters into their own hands.

Just before noon that day, Boyd Jones, the principal at Moton High, got a phone call. (The call had been secretly arranged by Barbara.) The caller warned that two of Jones's students were about to be arrested at the local bus station. Jones hurried to check it out.

As soon as Jones was gone, Barbara Johns sent four students around the school. Each one carried a note calling a school-wide meeting.

When the 450 students and teachers had gathered in the auditorium, the stage curtains parted to reveal Johns's student committee. Barbara stepped forward and banged her shoe on a bench. She insisted that the teachers leave, which they did.

Barbara then told the surprised student body that it was time to demand an education as good as any white student had. Everyone should walk out of school, she said. And they should stay out until equal treatment was on its way.

"It was a total surprise," recalled her sister Joanne Cobbs. "I should say, a total *shock*. And it was cause for fear. My parents were upset at first because they thought that there would be violence against Barbara and against the family."

In fact, there were plenty of reasons to be afraid. In the next county over, a school board member had threatened to "blow the brains out" of the first black kid who tried to enroll in a white school.

But that didn't stop Barbara. In fact, she took the protest a step further. She contacted the National Association for the Advancement of Colored People (NAACP). She knew the group was fighting school segregation in the South.

"We hate to impose," Barbara wrote, "but under the circumstances that we are facing, we have to ask for your help."

Two days later, NAACP lawyers Spotswood Robinson and Oliver Hill arrived in town.

The lawyers gathered 200 students and parents in a church basement. They wanted to make sure Prince Edward County was ready for the next step. Would the students move beyond their demand for a new school? *Were they willing to sue for the right to go to school with whites?*

"It seemed like reaching for the moon," Barbara Johns recalled. "It was all pretty hard to grasp."

But at a meeting the next day, the parents and students made a bold decision. They would sue to make segregated schools illegal in Virginia.

That summer, Barbara's family received threats from people who opposed school desegregation. Barbara went into hiding at her uncle's house in Montgomery, Alabama. She finished high school there.

Late in 1952, Barbara learned that her case would

be heard by the Supreme Court. It was grouped with four other cases. They all went under the name *Brown versus Board of Education of Topeka, Kansas.*

This case was finally decided on May 17, 1954, more than three years after Barbara Johns had cleared the halls at Moton High.

Segregation in public schools, the Supreme Court ruled, was unconstitutional.

Chief Justice Earl Warren wrote that education "is a right which must be made available to everyone on equal terms. No matter how good the separate schools were, segregation created conditions of inequality."

"To separate [blacks] from others . . . solely because of their race generates a feeling of inferiority," Warren wrote. And this feeling "may affect their hearts and minds in a way unlikely ever to be undone."

By the time the case was decided, Barbara Johns was living in Philadelphia. She had finished two years of college. She was married and raising a family. She had never been able to attend the kind of high school she had dreamed of. But thanks in part to her determination, thousands of kids in the South did.

How do you think Barbara Johns explained to her own kids her reasons for leading this protest?

He forced the world to realize that the rain forest in Brazil was going up in smoke.

CHICO MENDES

1944–1988

For months before the Christmas of 1988, Chico Mendes had expected to die. The warnings had come in various ways: an anonymous phone call, a tip from a stranger, a conversation overheard in a pool hall.

Friends had told him to stay away from his home on the Amazon River in eastern Brazil. But Chico had refused. For half his life he'd been helping several hundred thousand workers to protect their homes in the rain forest. He wasn't going to stop now.

"My blood is the same blood as that of these people suffering here," he told his sister. "I can't run away. This is the place where I will finish my mission."

And so he sat, on December 22, in his cottage in the village of Xapuri, playing dominoes with two bodyguards. Outside, the steady buzz of cicadas and the sounds of a popular TV show covered the movements of two men. They were dressed in dark jeans and carried shotguns. They set up behind the bushes in back of Chico's house. And they waited. . . .

For three generations, Chico Mendes's family had

made a living in the rain forest. They tapped huge trees for the sticky white sap known as latex rubber.

But as Chico was growing up, everything was beginning to change. The government of Brazil decided to develop the rain forest. And the tappers had to fight for their land and their way of life.

Chico became their leader. He risked his life to defend the tappers and preserve the rain forest. By December of 1988, people from London to New York knew the story of the Amazon rubber tappers . . . and the name of Chico Mendes.

For generations, families of tappers had lived off the rain forest without destroying it. They collected Brazil nuts in the rainy season. They used tree bark for torches. They boiled termite nests into a cough syrup and used countless other herbs and fruits for food and medicine.

But then the roads came. In the 1970s, the Brazilian government built modern roads deep into the jungle. Land that tappers had been using was sold. Soon the new owners were setting up ranches, mines, and farms. Thousands of tappers were forced out of the forest. Their huts were burned and their land was trampled by cattle.

In 1975, led by Chico Mendes, the tappers began to fight back. Chico hiked the thin trails between villages. He'd sit down with tappers, play with their children, ask questions, make friends. Then he'd call a meeting and talk about the need to get together and defend their way of life.

Before long, the tappers were going out in groups, armed with large, heavy knives called machetes. They would find the crews sent to clear the forest and confront them. They would take their camps apart and force the crews to go home. These *empates*, or stand-offs, would save about two million acres of rain forest over the next 12 years.

As the *empates* continued, life became dangerous for the tappers. Gunmen hired by the ranchers walked through the rain forest villages, pistols in their jeans. In December 1979, four hooded men forced Mendes into a car. They beat him up and dumped him on a darkened side street. By 1980, more than 100 Brazilians were dying in land disputes every year.

But Mendes and his struggle were about to become more than just local news. In 1986, Mendes met some Americans working to protect the environment. They convinced him to come to America to speak about what he had seen.

In March 1987, Mendes borrowed a gray suit, boarded a plane for Miami, and left his country for the first time in his life. Dressed in his wrinkled suit and wearing no tie, he sneaked into parties and told powerful leaders what was happening to the rain forest—and why they should care.

In just a decade, Mendes told them, ten percent of the Amazon rain forest had been cleared by fires and chain saws. These fires had become a serious threat to the earth. By the summer of 1987, a gray cloud of smoke the size of India hovered over Chico's homeland.

Scientists had begun to worry that the cloud was creating a "greenhouse effect." The theory was that gas from the smoke trapped heat near the earth. Over time, temperatures might rise enough to melt ice at the North and South Poles. Swelling oceans could flood New York City, Bangladesh, and entire island nations.

The destruction of the rain forest also threatened a huge number of plants and animals. A quarter of the medicines we use today contain some product of the rain forest. Scientists say that only one percent of the plants there have been studied for their health benefits. Was it possible that a cure for cancer was going up in smoke in Brazil?

When Chico Mendes came home from Miami, he was on his way to becoming famous. He traveled that summer to England and New York to accept awards for his work. The awards, he told a friend hopefully, would protect him from the ranchers.

But the dangers were growing every day. In April of 1988, Mendes forced a rancher named Darly Alves da Silva to give up 14,000 acres. The action saved two dozen families of tappers—and made Alves furious.

Rumors began to fly that Chico did not have long

to live. He sent faxes to leaders, naming the people who were planning to kill him. Brazilian police offered him two bodyguards. "Public gestures and a well-attended funeral will not save [the rain forest]," he said in one of his last interviews. "I want to live."

On the evening of December 22, Chico finished his game of dominoes. He grabbed a towel and headed out his back door to the outdoor shower. He had barely taken a step into the damp night when a shotgun blast split the air. At the age of 44, just a year-and-a-half after bringing the cause of the Amazon rubber tappers to the world, Chico Mendes was dead.

Mendes's death had a powerful impact. His funeral was packed with people from all over the world. Money began to pour into the tappers movement. A major highway through the rain forest was canceled. The Brazilian government protected 6,553 square miles of rain forest.

In 1991, Darly Alves da Silva was convicted of ordering Chico's death.

Why is the rain forest important to the tappers? Why is it important to the rest of the world?

CHIEF JOSEPH

Joseph was the leader of a large band of Nez Perce Indians. In 1877, soldiers chased them 1,700 miles. This photo was taken just before his death in 1904.

IRENE GUT OPDYKE

When World War II began, Opdyke was 18 years old. Her country, Poland, had been taken over by German soldiers. During the war, she stood up to the soldiers and risked her life to save 18 people.

During the war, these people worked in the German soldier's laundry in Tarnopol, Poland. This photo may include Opdyke and some Jewish workers she saved.

RACHEL CARSON

Carson first became known for her series of books about the mysteries of the ocean. She described the lives of fish, plants, and coral in a way that everyone could understand.

Carson's 1962 book, *Silent Spring*, shocked the world. It warned of the dangers of pesticides. The following year, she reported her findings to the U.S. Senate.

BARBARA JOHNS

Parents and students from Prince Edward County, Virginia, who took part in the court battles against segregation in the schools. This fight began in 1950, when one student, Barbara Johns, took a stand against the poor conditions in her all-black school.

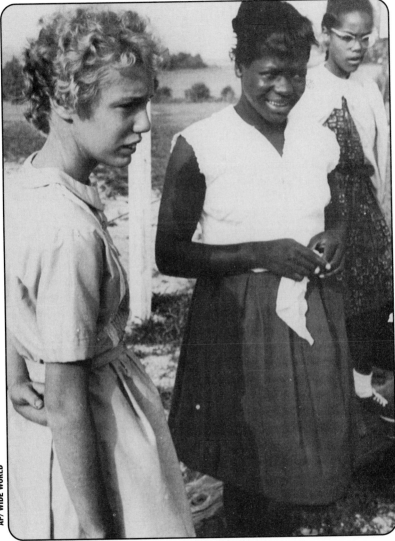

About 14 years after Barbara Johns's protests, black and white students in Prince Edward County began to go to school together. These students are among the first to attend an integrated school in that county.

Iqbal Masih

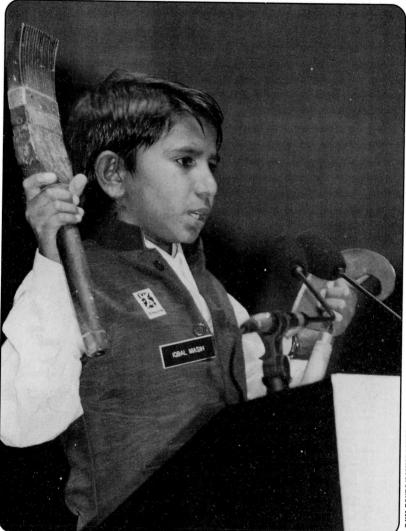

Iqbal devoted his life to protesting child labor. During
a 1994 trip to the U.S., he displayed tools used by
young children forced to work in a carpet factory.

When Iqbal came to the U.S., many people wanted to meet him—including musicians Michael Stipe of R.E.M., and Peter Gabriel.

Iqbal also met with American students to tell them about his experiences as a child laborer.

CHICO MENDES

Chico Mendes, activist in the Amazon rain forest, with his wife, Ilzamar Mendes, and their son Sandino, in 1988. Chico was killed later that year.

Chico Mendes (*right*), in front of the Farm Workers' Union headquarters in Xapuri, Brazil. The union fought for the rights of laborers in the rain forest.

The life and death of a young carpet maker inspired the world to stand up and fight against child labor.

IQBAL MASIH

1982–1995

When Iqbal Masih started going to work, he was too young to ride a bike. At age four, he had to get up before dawn to leave the two-room hut he shared with his mother and sister in Pakistan.

He would walk to a dusty carpet factory and take his place next to 20 other kids. Sometimes the factory owner would chain his leg to the loom, just to make sure he wouldn't run away.

There he would sit for the next 12 hours, tying knots into carpets until his fingers felt like they were falling off. Each carpet he made would be sent to Europe or America, where it would sell for hundreds of dollars. At the end of a week, Iqbal took home 20 cents, maybe 50 cents, if he was lucky.

The year was 1992. Astronauts were circling the earth in a space shuttle. Stockbrokers talked on cell phones the size of wallets. Kids in Europe and America played video games in the comfort of their own rooms.

Meanwhile, Iqbal Masih, at age ten, lived in slavery. And he wasn't the only one.

Around the world, about 200 million children worked instead of going to school. In Pakistan alone, eight million kids under the age of 15 had a story like Iqbal's. They worked 12 hours a day, six days a week stitching soccer balls and sneakers, molding bricks, or making carpets. In most cases, the parents needed the money desperately and the children didn't ask any questions.

Iqbal was different. He refused to accept his fate. And once he found a way out, he worked to free the kids who were still stuck behind the looms. He fought the system that had taken his freedom.

Iqbal never liked working. He wanted to play cricket or practice the kung-fu moves he'd seen in a movie once. But at first, he didn't have a choice.

His parents had needed 600 rupees—about $12—to pay for their older son's wedding. So they did what many poor Pakistani parents did. They sold their son's childhood for a small sum of money. They borrowed the 600 rupees from a factory owner and agreed that Iqbal would work at a loom until the debt was paid.

Iqbal's parents didn't realize that the debt would *never* be paid. Each month, the owner added more in fines or interest. Iqbal couldn't work hard enough to keep up. By the time Iqbal was ten, the owner claimed Iqbal's parents owed him 13,000 rupees.

As soon as he was old enough, Iqbal realized that

the system wasn't fair. He began to fight back however he could. Some days he would refuse to work overtime. Other days he would run away at lunchtime.

But each time the factory owner caught him, the punishments got worse. He was beaten, hung upside down, and burned with hot oil. Finally, he reported the abuses to the local police. They simply took him back to the carpet factory and handed him over.

At age ten, Iqbal found a way out. He made his way to a nearby city and went to a meeting of a group called the Bonded Labor Liberation Front (BLLF). The BLLF had freed thousands of child laborers in Pakistan, sometimes by raiding factories in broad daylight. It also ran dozens of schools around the country, where the children could learn to read and to work their way toward better jobs.

Iqbal stood up in the middle of the meeting and told his story. He was suffering from malnutrition. He stood under four feet tall and weighed less than 50 pounds. But hunger hadn't dimmed his desire for justice.

Iqbal learned that the practice of selling children to pay off debts had been made illegal. The law was rarely enforced. But legally, Iqbal was free and his parents cleared of their debt. He vowed never to return to the factory.

When he was ten years old, Iqbal went to school for the first time. He finished his classes in half the normal time. And he went on the road to share the most important lesson of all: No one has the right to enslave another human being.

Over the next two years, Iqbal hiked from factory to factory, telling children like himself that they had the right to be free. By the time he was 12, he had helped to free 3,000 kids.

Suddenly, the world noticed Iqbal. In December of 1994, he traveled to Boston, Massachusetts, to accept Reebok's Human Rights Youth in Action Award. He stood before a crowd of celebrities and journalists, holding a pen in one hand and a carpet weaving tool in another. "This," he said, pointing to the pen, "should be the tool of children everywhere, not this knife."

Iqbal returned home a new person. He had seen carpets on sale for more money than he'd made in six years of labor. He had spoken to children his age who spent their afternoons at malls and their weekends at the beach. He had been promised a full scholarship to college. And he had decided to become a lawyer.

Then, four months after his trip to the United States, Iqbal's dreams exploded with a single gunshot blast. On Easter Sunday he was gunned down while riding his bike near his grandmother's house. Police said the murderer was a drug addict. But human rights groups say Iqbal was killed by factory owners who wanted to silence his campaign against child labor.

"I used to be afraid of the carpet masters," Iqbal liked to tell reporters. "Now they are afraid of me."

Even in death, Iqbal gave them something to fear. Shortly after his murder, stories about child labor appeared in magazines and newspapers everywhere. Millions of people stopped buying products made with child labor. Carpet importers in Europe and America canceled $10 million in orders from Pakistan.

Iqbal's memory continues to inspire people around the world. Students at Broad Meadows Middle School in Quincy, Massachusetts, were so moved by a visit from Iqbal that they started their own campaign against child labor. In the year after Iqbal's death, they raised $80,000 to build schools in Pakistan.

Jim Cuddy, one of the student leaders at Broad Meadows, said Iqbal's story really made him appreciate his own life. "You never think about things," he said, "until something like Iqbal's death hits you."

What issues in your life or your community are important to you?

DID YOU LIKE THIS BOOK?

Here are two other READ 180
Paperbacks that you might like
to read.

THE BIG LIE
The true story of a young Jewish girl
trapped in Nazi-controlled Europe
during World War II.
ISABELLA LEITNER

STEALING HOME: THE STORY OF JACKIE ROBINSON
An exciting biography about the first
African-American baseball player to
play in the major leagues.
BARRY DENENBERG